CRIMINAL TERMINOLOGY

Crime and Detection series

- Criminal Terminology
- Cyber Crime
- Daily Prison Life
- Death Row and Capital Punishment
- Domestic Crime
- Famous Prisons
- Famous Trials
- Forensic Science
- Government Intelligence Agencies
- Hate Crimes
- The History and Methods of Torture
- The History of Punishment
- International Terrorism
- Major Unsolved Crimes
- Organized Crime
- Protecting Yourself Against Criminals
- Race and Crime
- Serial Murders
- The United States Justice System
- The War Against Drugs

CRIME AND DETECTION

CRIMINAL TERMINOLOGY

ELLEN DUPONT

MASON CREST PUBLISHERS
www.masoncrest.com

Mason Crest Publishers Inc.
370 Reed Road
Broomall, PA 19008
(866) MCP-BOOK (toll free)
www.masoncrest.com

First printing

1 2 3 4 5 6 7 8 9 10

Library of Congress Cataloging-in-Publication Data on file at the Library of Congress

ISBN 1-59084-383-5

Editorial and design by
Amber Books Ltd.
Bradley's Close
74–77 White Lion Street
London N1 9PF
www.amberbooks.co.uk

Project Editor: Michael Spilling
Design: Floyd Sayers
Picture Research: Natasha Jones

Printed and bound in Malaysia

CONTENTS

Introduction

From the moment in the Book of Genesis when Cain's envy of his brother Abel erupted into violence, crime has been an inescapable feature of human life. Every society ever known has had its own sense of how things ought to be, its deeply held views on how men and women should behave. Yet in every age there have been individuals ready to break these rules for their own advantage: they must be resisted if the community is to thrive.

This exciting and vividly illustrated new series sets out the history of crime and detection from the earliest times to the present day, from the empires of the ancient world to the towns and cities of the 21st century. From the commandments of the great religions to the theories of modern psychologists, it considers changing attitudes toward offenders and their actions. Contemporary crime is examined in its many different forms: everything from racial hatred to industrial espionage, from serial murder to drug trafficking, from international terrorism to domestic violence.

The series looks, too, at the work of those men and women entrusted with the task of overseeing and maintaining the law, from judges and court officials to police officers and other law enforcement agents. The tools and techniques at their disposal are described and vividly illustrated, and the ethical issues they face concisely and clearly explained.

All in all, the *Crime and Detection* series provides a comprehensive and accessible account of crime and detection, in theory and in practice, past and present.

CHARLIE FULLER

Executive Director, International Association of Undercover Officers

Left: Understanding criminal terminology, and how it is used by the judiciary, is an essential part of the process of law. Although legal jargon can seem mystifying to the layman, it is necessary for law courts to operate effectively.

Types of Crime

Since the first days of civilization, people have made rules to help them live together. These rules usually tell people how to behave, and often give the weak protection from the strong. In some societies, people believed these rules came from the gods; in other places, the ruler made the rules; while elsewhere, the community got together to make rules.

As time went on, societies began to write down the rules by which they lived. The first set of written rules we know of is the Code of Hammurabi from Babylon in 1800 B.C. Later, the Bible says that God gave Moses the Ten Commandments (around 1300 B.C.). Another famous set of laws, called the Edicts of Emperor Asoka, was produced in India in 250 B.C. Some fundamental ancient laws still form part of the rules we live by today—for example, the Fifth Commandment, "Thou shalt not kill."

WHAT IS A CRIME?

The term "crime" has been defined in many different ways. Some books describe it simply as anything that is against the law. Others explain it as something that is against the law and that harms or injures another person, or society as a whole. Other writers say it is something we are not allowed to do within our society. Some say it is actions that are harmful to society. Some crimes are the sort of thing that harms an individual, such as hitting a person. Others are crimes that harm society as a whole, such as cheating on your income tax return.

Criminal law covers all crimes against people and, by extension, society.

Left: Police arrest Scott LoBaid, 38, after he used an ax to behead an effigy of radical attorney Lynn Stewart in a one-man protest outside her office on Broadway in New York on April 17, 2002. Protests such as this are viewed as a breach of the peace by law enforcers.

An artist's impression published in the *Penny Illustrated Paper* of police discovering two more victims of Jack the Ripper in London's East End on September 30, 1888.

Because we do not want to live in a lawless society in which might is right, every wrong against one person is treated as a wrong against everyone in society. People do not have to defend themselves, because they have the police and the law on their side. Crimes against society include murder, theft, assault, **embezzlement**, abuse, and **arson**.

When a suspect is arrested, the police use handcuffs to restrain him or her. This practice is used by most law-enforcement agencies throughout the world.

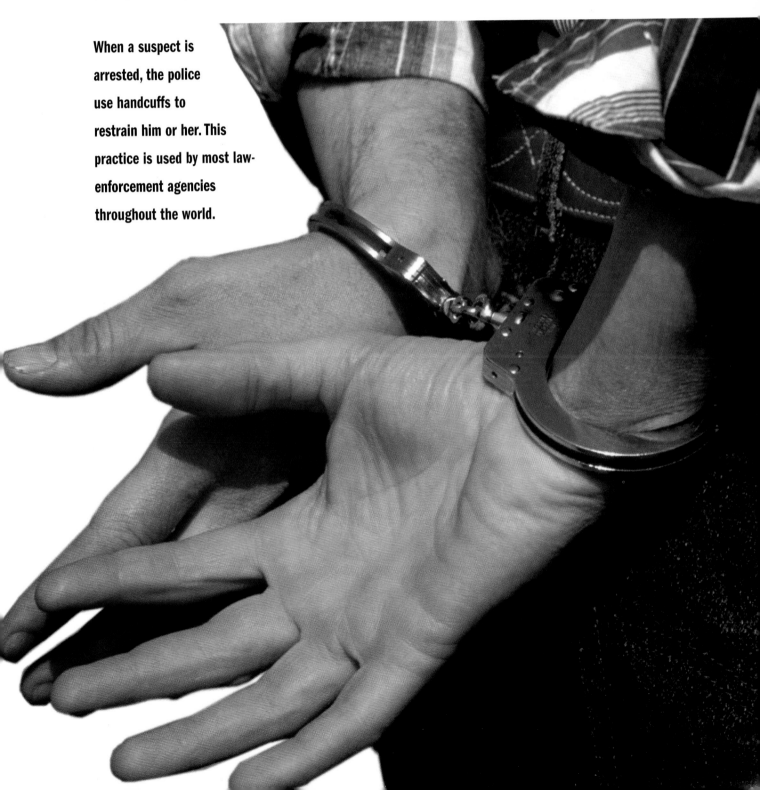

Since crimes are offenses against all of society, it is society, in the form of the state or the federal government, that brings the person who committed the crime to justice. That is why court cases are brought by the "People" or the "State." The decision to take the case to trial is made, not by the victim, but by the state prosecutor or district attorney. After the police have investigated a case and found a suspect, they offer the case to the prosecutor, who decides if it is strong enough to go to trial.

According to legal theorists, there are two basic kinds of law, those that are "*malum in se*," or wrong in themselves, and those that are "*malum prohibitum*," wrong because they are against a written law or statute. Murder, for example, is *malum in se*, while jaywalking, although not morally wrong, is *malum prohibitum* because it is against the laws that the government has made. In some cases, a crime can be committed by inaction as well as by an action. For example, some people, such as doctors, teachers, nurses, or clergy, are required to report suspected cases of child abuse. If they do not, they can be **fined**.

MAKING THE LAW

In the United States, there are literally thousands of different laws. They have been made by towns and cities, counties, the states, and the federal government. Local and county laws are specific to the place, outlawing drinking in public, for example. State laws, which are made by the state **legislature**, list what is against the law in that state; while the federal government has **jurisdiction** over matters that the Constitution has put under its control, such as interstate commerce.

These matters are set out in the Constitution and in the more than 900 statutes that have been passed by Congress. Cases that fall into this category are tried in federal courts. The federal district courts also have jurisdiction over income tax evasion. For many years, an infamous gangster, Al Capone, eluded prosecution for crimes of violence. He was finally convicted and sent to prison for income tax evasion.

The infamous gangster Al Capone eluded prosecution for crimes of violence, but he was finally convicted of income tax evasion and sent to prison.

This patrolman in Amherst, Massachusetts, is writing out a speeding ticket after catching someone doing 53 mph (83 kph) in a 40 mph (64 kph) zone. The majority of crimes committed every day are of a minor nature, like speeding or illegal parking.

Crimes are divided by how serious they are. The least serious crimes are violations, or infractions. They include things like parking tickets. The only penalty for these offenses is a fine. **Misdemeanors**—for example, shoplifting something worth less than a certain amount—are more serious and carry a penalty of less than one year in jail. Felonies, including murder, are the most serious crimes and carry a penalty of more than one year in jail, up to life imprisonment or even the death penalty.

Laws are made by our elected representatives at the local, state, and federal levels. When a law is passed, it is written down and put into the statute books, where anyone can look it up. The statutes define the crime, listing its elements. For a person to be guilty of a particular crime, all the elements must be present. If they are not all present, the person cannot be found guilty of that particular crime. For example, there are many crimes in the category of theft, larceny, or robbery. The prosecutor must decide which particular statute fits the circumstances of the crime. The case will then be prosecuted on this basis.

VIOLATIONS

Called petty offenses, citations, infractions, or violations, depending on the area of the United States, these crimes are fairly minor. They include traffic and parking offenses, littering, disturbing the peace, trespassing, and loitering. For some of these offenses, you will get a ticket rather than being arrested. Others, such as disturbing the peace, may result in an arrest. The penalty is usually a fine under a certain amount that varies from state to state. If this is not paid, a short jail sentence may be handed down.

For some minor offenses, the police need to prove only that you committed the offense. They do not need to show that you intended to commit it. For example, if you are speeding and the police catch you on their radar, explaining that your speedometer was broken, or that you did not know what the speed limit was, will not help. Even if you were merely careless or negligent, you are still guilty of the offense.

AIDING AND ABETTING

Even if someone did not actually commit a crime, he or she might be guilty of a crime because he or she helped another person to commit, or get away with, a crime. In these circumstances, being present when a crime is committed can be an offense. Thus, a person who went along with friends and intentionally aided in the stealing of a car would be charged with the same crime even if she did not steal the car herself.

MISDEMEANORS

Misdemeanors include some assaults, shoplifting an inexpensive item, simple theft, trespassing, battery (hitting or touching someone with the intent to harm him or her), public indecency, and phone harassment. Misdemeanors are punishable by a fine or time in jail, up to a maximum of one year. The judge can also hand down a sentence of community service, perhaps making a litterbug volunteer to help clean the streets, or a thief give a certain amount of money to charity.

Regularly committing the same misdemeanor can escalate the penalty so that it is more than one year in jail; that is, the defendant is sentenced as though he had committed a **felony**. For example, in most states, drunk driving is a misdemeanor, but in some states, after being convicted of drunk driving more than a certain number of times, the potential punishment becomes much more severe. Some states have what is known as persistent-offender laws, or the "three strike law," which allows a more severe penalty if the defendant is found guilty of the same offense three times.

FELONIES

The most serious crimes against society are classified as felonies. These crimes are punishable by lengthy jail terms, which can range from one year

Many stores use security cameras to catch shoplifters. The videotape is then used as evidence in court to prosecute the shoplifter.

This driver is taking a sobriety test. The police officer has asked him to walk a straight line to prove that he is not over the legal alcohol limit. Police officers may also use breathalizers to test the level of alcohol in the suspect's bloodstream.

to life imprisonment. In addition, people convicted of a felony can lose some of their rights, including the right to vote, the right to own a gun, and the right to serve on a jury. The punishment for some felonies is death. Felonies include murder, manslaughter, rape, sexual assault, arson, forgery, home invasion, theft, and stalking.

To be convicted of a felony, the prosecutor must prove that someone not only committed the crime, but also that he or she intended to commit the crime. This is called the motive. So long as intention is present, the offender need not have known that what he or she was doing was a crime. Ignorance of the law is not a defense. For example, in most states, it is a crime for an adult to have consensual sexual intercourse with a person under 16 years old. This crime is called "statutory rape," and the adult can be found guilty even if the person under 16 looked much older.

HOMICIDE

In the law, the unlawful killing of one person by another is called homicide. With some important exceptions, such as a police officer killing someone in the line of duty or being accidentally responsible for a death, causing the death of another person is a crime. But the type of crime depends upon the circumstances and the state of mind of the person who caused the death. Homicides are graded by how vicious they are and whether or not they were planned, unplanned, or accidental. Murder in the first degree is the most serious form of homicide, while homicide by misadventure is not a crime because, although a death resulted, no harm was intended. If, however, the death was caused because the defendant was much less careful or cautious than a reasonable person ought to be, the defendant might be guilty of criminally negligent homicide.

Murder is the most serious form of homicide. To commit murder, the murderer must have killed someone and must have intended to kill that person. All states divide the crime of murder into different categories. Usually, in murder in the first degree, torture, poisoning, or some other aggravating factor is involved. If the murder was committed while the murderer was committing another crime, such as armed robbery, the charge would be murder in the first degree, or felony murder. Murder in the second degree is sometimes called manslaughter.

If the killer did not intend to kill the other person, he or she might be charged with, or found guilty of, a lesser crime, such as criminal homicide or manslaughter. In the crime of manslaughter, the killer was acting unlawfully, but did not intend to kill the victim. It is not necessarily premeditated (meaning it was planned). Voluntary manslaughter is the result of a wrongful act, such as punching someone in a fight. Involuntary manslaughter is the result of a lawful act that was carried out without due care, such as one boxer killing another during a fight by punching him in a way that is against the rules of the ring.

MURDER IN SELF-DEFENSE

Killing someone in self-defense is excusable, or justifiable, homicide. However, not all killings in which the killer was protecting herself would be classed as justifiable homicide. The killer must have been in fear for her life and must have used reasonable force. It is up to the police, and eventually the courts, to decide if the circumstances of the killing make it justifiable homicide or not. For example, imagine someone has broken into your house. You shout at him to get out or you will call the police, and then shoot him in the back as he is running away. This killing would not be considered self-defense because you were not in fear for your life at the time you fired the shot.

Negligent homicide occurs when someone has done something wrong, but without intending to cause harm, which then contributes to or results in someone's death. For example, a homeowner fills her pool with only two feet of water and places a diving board at the pool, thereby causing the death of someone that dove into such shallow water.

Sometimes, one person is responsible for another's death, but did not

This man is held by homicide detectives after stabbing a security guard in a brawl at a nightclub. Homicide detectives are called if the victim is dead or likely to die. Luckily, in this case, the stabbed man survived.

intend to kill that person. In that case, a verdict of not guilty should result because that person was acting within the law and killed someone else without meaning to do so. For example, if a child ran out from between two parked cars and the driver could not stop in time, despite being within

Police and emergency personnel attend a four-car accident in Jacksonville, Illinois. The police are required to go to any accident that might involve injury or death.

In London, England, a police officer arrests a man for streaking at a public event. The man is committing an offense in an attempt to draw attention to a political cause.

the speed limit and obeying all traffic rules, the driver would not be guilty of negligent homicide if the child died. If, however, the driver was speeding or was drunk, the charge would be vehicular homicide (also called negligent homicide with a motor vehicle) and the penalty could be severe. Sometimes, one person is responsible for another's death, but did not intend to kill that person. In that case, a verdict of homicide by misadventure, or excusable, or justifiable, homicide might be handed down.

Usually, in order to be tried for murder, there must be a dead body, or a *corpus delecti*. In a famous Connecticut case, called the "Wood-Chipper Trial," the defendant was tried and found guilty of a murder without a body. The defendant rented a wood-chipper and chopped his wife's body in it and then dumped the chips into a lake. Based on evidence given by **forensic** pathologist Dr. Henry Lee, the jury found that the defendant's wife had been murdered.

THE ROLE OF CIRCUMSTANTIAL EVIDENCE: THE LINDBERGH BABY CASE

On March 1, 1932, the 20-month-old baby son of famous aviator Charles Lindbergh and his wife, author Anne Morrow Lindbergh, was kidnapped. The only evidence was a ransom note found on the windowsill and a handmade wooden ladder leaning against the wall of the house.

For nearly two months, a go-between negotiated with the kidnapper through anonymous advertisements in the newspapers. Ransom money was paid for the safe return of the baby, some of it in gold certificates, some in cash, but the baby was not where the kidnapper said he would be. Finally, on May 12, 1932, the baby's body was discovered partially buried about four miles away from the Lindberghs' home. He had been dead for two months.

The FBI and the New Jersey police embarked on an extensive manhunt for the killer. They used an artist's impression of the kidnapper and speech and handwriting analysis, as well as analysis of the wood and building methods used in the ladder. They also tracked gold certificates, looking for those given to the kidnapper. In September 1934, they finally found the man who had been passing the Lindbergh gold certificates. He was Bruno Richard Hauptmann (see picture opposite, center).

Hauptmann resembled the artist's impression, and his handwriting matched the ransom notes. He was a carpenter by trade. Wood from the ladder matched wood in his attic, while his tools matched tool marks on the ladder. The go-between's name and phone number were written on the inside of a closet in his house. He owned shoes that had been purchased with a Lindbergh gold receipt. All of this was circumstantial evidence, but together, it convinced the jury.

The court convicted him of the baby's murder, and he was sentenced to death. On April 3, 1936, he was electrocuted.

Police Procedure

It is the job of the police, sometimes called the thin blue line, to prevent crime, to protect society from people who break the law, to solve crimes when they happen, and to testify in court about the crimes. There are over one million law enforcement officials in the United States, working for 40,000 different local, county, and state police departments. It is their duty to enforce local, state, and federal laws. In carrying out this duty, police officers perform a wide range of different tasks.

GUARDIANS OF THE PUBLIC PEACE

These include identifying suspects, investigating crimes, making arrests, testifying at trials, deterring crime by patrolling the streets, helping members of the public, giving emergency aid, resolving conflicts between people, keeping the peace, directing traffic, and operating the police departments for which they work. Not all of these jobs are exciting or even dangerous. A lot of time is spent doing paperwork and filling in forms. Deterring crime and making the community feel safe by patrolling the streets, either on foot or more commonly in a squad car, is another important part of police work.

The Supreme Court summed up the role of the police in the case of *United States v. Allen* (1973): "The local policeman...is also in a very real sense a guardian of the public peace, and has a duty in the course of his work to be alert for suspicious circumstances and, provided that he acts within constitutional limits, to investigate whenever such circumstances indicate to him that he should do so."

Left: A police officer's duties may include crowd control at sports events, political rallies, and other social events. This officer is providing security inside the stadium for a NFL game at the Rose Bowl in Pasadena, California.

These police officers are policing a protest march during the World Economic Forum in New York on February 2, 2002. The officers' helmets have riot shields to protect their faces in case they are attacked.

The police are governed in what they can legally investigate and how they can investigate it by the Constitution, in particular, the Bill of Rights. They must respect the suspect's constitutional rights. If they do not, some or all of the evidence that they collect will not be admissible in court, possibly causing the case to collapse. They are also governed by their state constitutions, which may afford suspects greater rights than the U.S. Constitution itself.

Computers are now an essential piece of equipment for police departments. This computer in the Jacksonville, Illinois, police department's communications room is linked to the Law Enforcement Agency Data System, and provides information on driver's licences and criminal records.

THE ORGANIZATION OF A POLICE DEPARTMENT

All police departments are organized along similar lines, based on the organization of military forces. An officer's rank indicates his or her position within the force and the level of authority he or she has. The head of the department is the chief of police. The police chief is in charge of the entire department, and everyone in the department reports to him or her either directly or indirectly. Other ranks are: lieutenant colonel, major, captain, lieutenant, sergeant, corporal, and private. These are the same ranks found in the armed forces.

Within the department, there is a clear chain of command, with each officer reporting to his or her superior. So a desk sergeant would report to

This suspect was carrying a gun. While the officer examines the weapon, which turned out to be a fake, the suspect kneels in front of him with his hands clasped behind his neck.

POLICE TRANSPORTATION

In addition to cars, the police use many other kinds of transportation. Depending on the terrain and the area, motorcycles, dune buggies, snowmobiles, boats, bicycles, and dogsleds have all been used by U.S. police departments. Planes and helicopters are also used. Helicopters are particularly useful for surveillance since they can hover over a suspicious area and even light it up at night.

The police use cars to patrol our cities and towns. They can move quickly and cover large distances, but in a car, the officers do not have as much contact with people as patrolmen on a beat, and this can make their role a bit impersonal.

a lieutenant, who would report to a captain, and so on.

Work within a police department is divided into line and non-line jobs. The line officers are in direct contact with the public. They include officers on the beat and detectives working on cases. Non-line employees, some of whom are police officers and some are not, give administrative and technical support to the line officers. People that collect and analyze evidence, such as polygraph examiners, photographers, fingerprint and crime scene technicians, and people doing forensic work in police laboratories, have non-line jobs, as do those who provide administrative services, such as typing, filing, and answering the phone.

The daily activities of a police officer vary according to the size of the department in which he or she works. In a small town employing less than 20 police officers (about 80 percent of U.S. police departments fall into this category), the officers will perform a wide variety of tasks, from arresting suspects to investigating cases to writing parking tickets. In a big city, an individual officer's job is likely to be more specialized.

DIVISIONS OF DUTY AND PATROLS

City police forces are usually divided into a number of divisions, such as traffic, detectives, juvenile, **vice**, and patrol. Officers working in these divisions specialize in one area and generally work on crimes only within that area. Of course, a member of the vice squad who would normally deal with crimes involving prostitution, narcotics, and gambling can still write a traffic ticket, while a member of the traffic department would make a narcotics arrest upon witnessing a drug deal.

Within a division, there are squads, such as the Robbery Squad, which deal with a particular type of crime. These groups are further broken down into teams, which can be either a pair of officers or a group working on a particular case or project. Time is divided into eight-hour periods called watches or shifts.

A police department is also divided into geographic areas. The police

Here, officers are patrolling an inner-city neighborhood in the Bronx, one of New York City's five boroughs. In cities, officers on foot are the eyes and ears of the police department. Patrolling on foot also lets them get to know the people on their "beat."

chief and the central administration are based in the headquarters, also known as HQ. In a small town, this is usually just called the police station. Large cities are divided into districts or precincts, and these are then subdivided into beats. Within the beats, there are posts (particular places, such as street intersections and surveillance points) and routes (busy, main streets that are patrolled regularly).

Police patrols are an important part of law enforcement. Foot patrols are common in high-crime urban areas. In rural and suburban areas, they

The police do not work alone in solving crimes. Here, an arson investigator from the fire marshall's office inspects the site of a suspicious fire. If he discovers that the fire was started deliberately, the police will investigate the crime.

This policeman is apprehending a suspect while his partner radios in to let headquarters know what is happening.

would be inefficient, so cars are used instead. Although there used to be two officers in a car, there is now usually only one because of budget cuts. By patrolling the same beat, the officers get to know it and people get to know them, which makes it easier for them to spot or find out about crime.

INVESTIGATING A CRIME

A crime is a wrong committed against the community as defined by local, state, or federal law. The police can find out about a crime in three main ways: they can see it happen; they can hear about it from the victim or another member of the public; or they can find evidence of it (such as a dead body). After they have learned of a crime, they investigate and collect evidence and, once they have identified a suspect, make an arrest.

When someone has been the victim of the crime, that person usually makes a complaint to the police. For example, if someone's purse has been snatched, the victim calls the police to report the theft. An officer is then sent out to take a crime report, or the victim may be asked to go to the police station to swear a complaint. The officer will take a detailed statement about what happened, asking for a description of the robber, details of what was stolen, the place and time the incident occurred, and anything else the victim can remember, such as a suspicious car or person loitering nearby.

If the victim had fought back and perhaps injured the robber, the police would go back to the scene of the crime to look for evidence from the struggle, such as blood or footprints. An important part of investigating a crime is securing the place where the crime took place (the crime scene). The police cordon off and guard the crime scene until they have collected all the evidence they can. They do not want the scene to be contaminated, by, for example, other people walking over it, leaving fingerprints, dropping things, or picking up evidence and taking it away.

If the police find someone in that area answering to the robber's description, they may stop and question him. The police can stop and question anyone if they have reason to believe that he or she is involved in criminal activity. The Supreme Court has handed down a number of decisions about the circumstances under which the police can stop people. There must be a good reason; they cannot stop everyone in a certain neighborhood, for example. The more detailed the victim's description of the attacker is and the more unusual-looking the suspect is, the more likely the officer will have reasonable grounds to stop and search him. The description "a white man in a dark windbreaker with the hood up" fits many people, so the police could not reasonably stop everyone fitting that description. If, however, the assailant is described as a white man in a dark windbreaker with the hood up and a large red, waxed handlebar mustache,

THE STRUCTURE OF A POLICE STATION

Within the police station, there are a number of different areas. One, the complaint or information desk, is open to the public. This is where people come to report a crime or ask for or give information. It is usually at the front of the building. At the back of the building is the station desk, staffed by a desk sergeant. Suspects are brought in through this entrance so that they can be booked. Inside the station, there are a number of other rooms. How many depends on the size of the police department or station. These rooms might include some or all of the following: a briefing room where roll call is taken at the beginning of each shift, holding cells where suspects are kept, an evidence room, an interview room, a room where officers can do paperwork, and offices for the squads or officers based at the station. Some police stations have rooms for victims of crimes. Others have special rooms, called rape suites, for examining and interviewing victims of sexual attacks.

This officer holds handcuffs and two plastic bags of crack cocaine. During an arrest, the officer will use the handcuffs to restrain the suspect until they reach the police station.

the police could reasonably stop someone fitting that description, since it would fit few people.

MAKING AN ARREST

The rules governing arrest are complex and are regulated by what is allowed under the Constitution. The Fourth Amendment governs what the police can do in an arrest, as well as in a search of a person's property. It states:

"The right of the people to be secure in their persons, houses, papers, and effects, against unreasonable searches and seizures, shall not be violated, and no Warrants shall issue, but upon probable cause, supported by Oath or affirmation, and particularly describing the place to be searched, and the persons or things to be seized."

These police officers are arresting a suspected drug dealer. In order to enter the home and make the arrest, they must usually either be in hot pursuit of the suspect or have a warrant that authorizes them to make a specific arrest.

Over the years, the Supreme Court has made many rulings clarifying and explaining what this one long sentence means. As regards arrest, the main point is that there should be probable cause to make the arrest. Probable cause means having a good reason to suspect someone of criminal activity. A good reason is not a guess or a hunch; it is a series of trustworthy facts that would convince a reasonable person.

The police can make an arrest if they actually see someone committing a crime—for example, if they witness one person stealing another's wallet. In other cases, such as arresting a person in his or her own home, the police need an arrest warrant to make an arrest. An arrest warrant is a document signed by a judge specifying who is to be arrested, what the probable cause is, and what the person is to be charged with.

In certain cases, the police can make an arrest without a warrant and without actually seeing the crime committed. These arrests often come about when a police officer has reason to suspect someone of involvement in a crime. In that case, he or she can stop a person briefly for questioning. This is called a stop and frisk. During the stop, the officer can ask the person questions. He or she can also **frisk** the person to check for weapons. If the officer feels a hard metallic object, which might be a gun, he or she can remove it from the suspect's pocket. If it turns out to be a canister containing drugs, the police officer has the power to make an arrest since the drugs were found during a legitimate search. If, however, the officer felt a soft pouch, an item that could not possibly be used as a weapon, he would have no right to take it out of the person's pocket, even if he suspected that the package contained drugs. If the officer did take out the package and even if it was found to contain drugs, it could probably not be used as evidence in court because it was taken improperly. Other arrests without a warrant might come about when police are doing routine checks looking for drunk drivers. For example, if they stopped a car and smelled marijuana, they would have reason to make a more thorough search of the car. If they found drugs, they could then make an arrest.

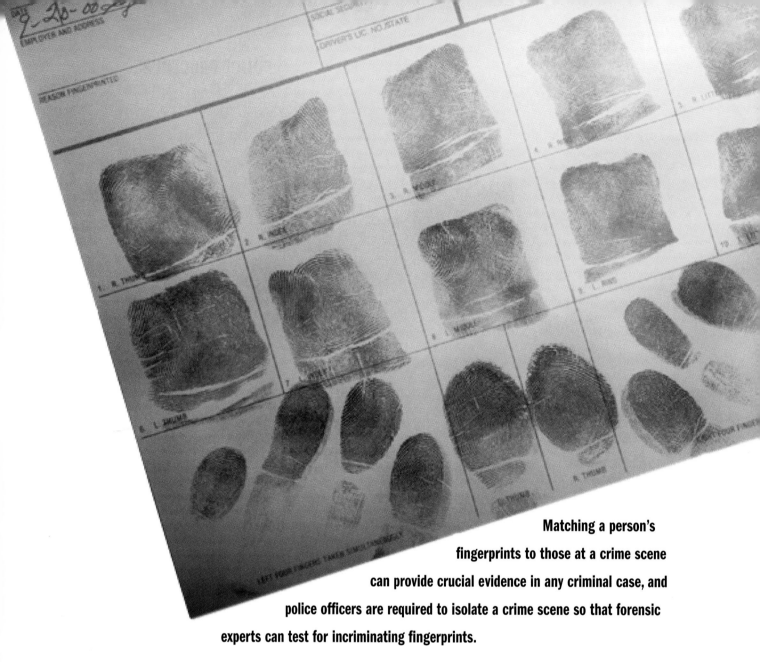

Matching a person's fingerprints to those at a crime scene can provide crucial evidence in any criminal case, and police officers are required to isolate a crime scene so that forensic experts can test for incriminating fingerprints.

READING YOUR RIGHTS

The police often say, "You are under arrest," when they arrest someone. However, if the police hold someone against his or her will, this counts as an arrest even if the police do not formally say so. Once someone is under arrest, he must be informed of his rights. The suspect's constitutional rights, called Miranda rights, were outlined in the Supreme Court decision *Miranda v. Arizona.* Usually, the police read out a list of rights, such as:

"You have the right to remain silent. If you do say anything, what you say can be used against you in a court of law. You have the right to consult with a lawyer and to have that lawyer present during any questioning. If you cannot afford a lawyer, one will be appointed for you if you so desire.

If you choose to talk to the police officer, you have the right to stop the interview at any time."

If the police do not inform the suspect of his or her rights when they arrest him or her, anything he or she says is inadmissible—that is, it cannot be used in court. Any evidence collected on the basis of these statements is also inadmissible due to a doctrine called "Fruit of the Poisonous Tree." This doctrine says that anything that is the result of an illegal search or illegal questioning is also inadmissible.

Once the police have arrested a suspect, they often arrange a lineup to see if the victim can identify him. A lineup is a group of people who all look similar to the suspect. They stand in a line and the victim looks through a two-way mirror and is asked if she can identify the attacker. In small towns, photographic lineups are common. The victim is shown a collection of photographs of similar-looking people, including the suspect, and asked to identify her assailant. When only the suspect is shown to the victim, it is called a show-up. This form of identification is not as

Police officers on the beat get to know local people. When a crime occurs, they can ask them if they have heard who might have done it.

convincing in court as that made in a lineup, since the fact that a suspect has been picked up by the police may influence the victim.

COLLECTING EVIDENCE

Collecting evidence is an important part of police work. As with arrests, evidence must be collected according to procedures indicated in the Fourth Amendment and expanded upon by the Supreme Court. The Fourth Amendment is intended to protect people from unreasonable actions by the police, such as arresting them, taking their property, or entering their

Passersby can sometimes provide valuable information about a crime. Here, an officer talks to a man after an explosion at a technical school in New York City.

THE MUG BOOK

Crime victims are often taken to the police station to look through the mug book to see if they can recognize the assailant. The mug book contains police photographs (known as mug shots) of people who have been arrested in that area. If the victim identifies someone from the book, the police will investigate further and might question him or her.

homes without good reason. The police must have probable cause to make an arrest, carry out a search, or seize property. Probable cause means a good reason that can be explained in words and that can be backed up by facts.

Generally, the police need permission either from the owner or occupant of the property they plan to search or from a judge to enter a building and collect evidence. Permission from a judge comes in the form of a search warrant. To get a search warrant, the police must fill in a form indicating what probable cause they have for believing they will find evidence during the search. They must say exactly what they are looking for and where they plan to look for it. It is up to the judge to decide if this is a reasonable request. If she thinks it is, she will sign the warrant and the officers can proceed with the search.

There are some circumstances under which the police can make a search without a warrant. The purpose of the Fourth Amendment was to protect people's privacy, so a warrant is usually needed only to make a search of private places. A warrant is not needed to search public places or things that are generally open to public inspection. For example, the police can search a car if they see a gun in the front seat. They can search an open field or garbage that has been left on the street. If they see something illegal from the street, such as a marijuana plant in the window, they can search the room the plant is in, but not the rest of the house. However, if, while they

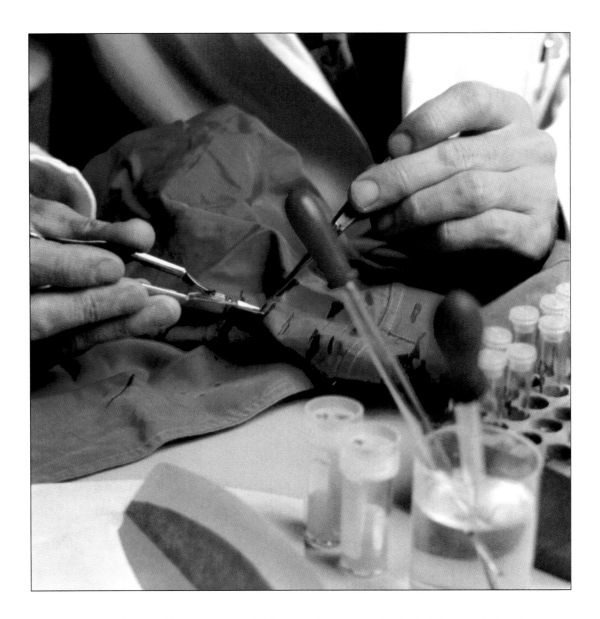

Thanks to the science of forensics, bloodstains on clothing can be tested to reveal who the blood came from. Using this kind of evidence lets police link suspects to victims or to the scene of a crime.

are searching that one room, something happens to make them think evidence is being destroyed in another part of the house, such as a toilet flushing upstairs, they may search elsewhere.

Sometimes, evidence comes from the suspect's own body. When a suspect is arrested, the police may be entitled to take what is called physical-trait evidence. For many years, most suspects had only their photograph and fingerprints taken. In some cases, the police can also take samples of blood, breath, hair, fingernails, and urine, as well as handwriting and voice samples. In addition, the police can look for physical evidence, such as scratches or injuries, or identifying marks, such as scars and tattoos, forcing the suspect to undress if necessary. The police can also search a suspect's body cavities if they have reason to believe something is hidden there. They can also make the suspect spit out anything he is holding in his mouth. They cannot, however, pump the suspect's stomach even if they have reason to believe drugs are hidden there.

Administration and paperwork make up a large part of a police officer's job. These officers finishing a shift in Syracuse, New York, are completing paperwork before going home.

This officer is examining several small bags of crack cocaine as he stands by his police car. Police officers have to be trained to identify the various types of drugs they can encounter when dealing with suspected criminals.

FORENSIC EVIDENCE

Evidence gathered at the scene of the crime can be used to help the police find out what happened and who committed the crime. For many years, the police have used fingerprints to prove that a suspect was present at a crime scene. The FBI keeps a computerized national database of fingerprints, which has fingerprints from more than 79 million people on it. Many of these are from law-abiding citizens, while others are from convicted criminals. Using computers, the police can rapidly find out if a suspect's fingerprints match any of those in the FBI's database.

Advances in technology are giving law enforcement officials ever more sophisticated crime-solving tools. For many years, all that could be said of a blood sample was what type the blood was. However, that evidence was of little use in proving whose blood it was, since over half of the population shares the most common blood type. All it could prove conclusively was whose blood it was not. The discovery of DNA and the acceptance of DNA evidence in court have now made it possible to prove almost beyond a shadow of doubt that a blood sample comes from a particular individual. DNA can be collected from tiny samples of an individual's blood or saliva. There is enough DNA left on the back of a stamp that someone has licked to provide a conclusive match.

Thanks to DNA evidence, many old murder cases have been solved. Bloodstained clothing and skin taken from underneath the victim's fingernails have been tested and, in some cases, have matched individuals in police databases, enabling them to be tried and convicted even 20 or 30 years later.

The police have many different tools with which to solve crimes. They can use portable lasers, scanning **electron microscopes**, and ultraviolet light to look for evidence that is not visible to the naked eye.

CHARGING A SUSPECT

Once evidence has been gathered and someone has been arrested, he or she is taken to the police station and charged with the crime. The police decide what to charge the person with based on a knowledge of the law. Theft, for example, is covered by a number of different laws, which are described in the statute books. Different elements make up each crime. For example, the crime of grand theft auto is made up of the following elements: taking a car without the owner's permission with the intention of keeping or selling it. When charging someone with grand theft auto, the police must make sure all those elements are present. If the car was taken, but the thief did not intend to keep it, he or she might be charged with a lesser crime relating to the theft of the car. Even at the trial, the charge can be reduced. The jury may find the defendant not guilty of the crime of grand theft auto, but guilty of some lesser crime of auto theft. Once the jury has determined that the defendant did not commit the greater crime, the judge will tell (instruct) the jury which lesser crimes it may consider.

Once someone has been arrested, he or she is taken to court and charged. The police may continue to investigate the case to gather more evidence, and they will probably be called to appear in court to testify against the suspect, now known as the defendant.

POLICE SLANG

Like any group of people, the police have developed their own private language, a sort of shorthand for referring to common events and procedures. Sometimes, this can be as simple as referring to something by its initials. A "modus operandi," the criminal's typical way of doing things, is often called an "m.o.," while "also known as" is often referred to as "a.k.a." and "D.O.A." means "dead on arrival."

Sometimes, words are shortened, so "perpetrator" becomes "perp." Drug users and vagrants may be called "skels," short for skeletons, since many of them are quite thin.

Areas and jobs within the police force have nicknames, not all of them complimentary. These include rat squad (internal affairs), white shirts (police management), loo (lieutenant), and DT (detective). The police station may be called "the house."

Other times, the slang is a kind of in-joke, so officers might say that a suspect whom they claimed had dropped a bag of drugs had "dropsy," or

Before getting out of his unit (car) to tackle an armed Code 5 (wanted person), the R.O. (responding officer) would have phoned in a Code 8 (report of a critical situation) or a Ten-One (request for emergency backup).

they might talk about "testilying" instead of testifying to indicate that the perpetrator was not telling the truth in court.

When the police talk on the radio, they often use "10" codes, a combination of the number 10 and other numbers. These codes, the most famous of which is 10-4, meaning affirmative, or OK, enable them to convey information quickly. Although the Association of Public Safety Communications Officials has an official listing of these terms, many police departments have developed their own "10" codes, which may not be the same.

The Language of the Courts

A criminal case is brought by the state or federal government against someone accused of committing a criminal offense. Offenses are divided into four categories: infractions, violations, misdemeanors, and felonies. Both federal and state crimes are divided into the same categories. Infractions include minor motor vehicle offenses. Violations are minor offenses, such as littering, for which the usual punishment is a fine. Misdemeanors are less serious than felonies, and the penalty is a sentence of less than one year in jail. Felonies are crimes that carry a penalty of more than one year in jail. Federal crimes are violations of federal law.

THE JOB OF THE JUDGE

All criminal cases are tried in the trial courts, either in courts of limited jurisdiction or in courts of general jurisdiction, depending on the severity of the offense. Federal crimes are tried in the federal courts. Despite the many different rules and procedures, all courts are run in similar ways.

The judge presides over the case. The judge's job is to decide points of law and to make sure both sides present their cases in an orderly way and according to the appropriate rules. The judge also instructs the jury about the law.

In some cases, defendants decide not to have a jury trial and choose to

Left: This police officer is testifying about a gun that has been entered in evidence at a criminal trial. Police officers must be present to identify evidence at the trial and to answer questions about it. Meanwhile, the jury looks at a photograph of the gun on a computer screen.

let the judge hear the case alone. This is called a bench trial. Defendants choose bench trials when the issues are complicated, perhaps involving scientific questions or accounting, or if they think the jury will become too emotionally involved in the case. It is unusual to have a bench trial in a criminal case.

The prosecution in a criminal case is the state, sometimes called "The People." A crime is an offense against the state, not against the victim of the crime; the victim appears in court only as a witness for the prosecution. In some states, the victim may also appear in court to provide input as to the appropriate sentence if the defendant is convicted. The person in charge

The judge is in charge in the courtroom. As well as making legal rulings, he keeps order and may bang his gavel to get everyone's attention if feelings become heated.

In the opening and closing arguments in any court trial, the lawyers for both sides speak directly to the jury as they argue the case. The lawyers summarize the case and attempt to influence the jury's decision.

of the prosecution's case is the public prosecutor in a city or the state's district attorney (often referred to by the initials "D.A.") or a member of his or her staff.

THE DEFENSE

The person accused of the crime is known as the defendant. Defendants have a constitutional right to legal representation and if they cannot afford a lawyer, the state must provide one free of charge. This is usually through the public defender's office. A court-appointed lawyer will represent someone free of charge if he or she cannot afford to pay. State and county bar associations often provide lists of lawyers who will work for a minimal fee for those on a low income.

The strategy of the defense is to show why the defendant could not have committed the crime or why the prosecution's evidence is either weak or invalid. The defense might claim that there is insufficient evidence to prove the defendant's guilt beyond a **reasonable doubt**. Or, he or she might try to prove that the defendant's rights were violated during the course of the police investigation, thus making some or all of the evidence inadmissible.

Other common defenses are alibi, mistaken identity, entrapment, and self-defense. For example, the defendant may have an alibi—some proof that he or she was someplace else at the time the crime was committed. A mistaken-identity defense will try to show that witnesses may have mistakenly identified the defendant, perhaps because it was too dark to see clearly. In an entrapment defense, the defense will claim that the person would not have committed the offense if he had not been lured to do so by the police. This defense is most common in vice-related offenses, in which police decoys pose as drug dealers or prostitutes.

If self-defense is claimed, then the defense will try to show that the defendant was in fear for his life and struck out in self-defense. If the defense is insanity, the defendant agrees that he committed the crime, but says he is not guilty because, due to his mental state, he could not tell the difference between right and wrong. Whatever strategy the defense chooses, before the case goes to trial, the defense lawyer gathers evidence and decides which witnesses to call in support of the case.

THE JURY

In the United States, everyone has a right to trial by jury. If the defendant chooses to have a jury trial, the judge decides legal issues, but the jury decides whether or not the defendant is guilty.

Jury selection is the first step. During *voir dire* (pronounced "vwar deer"), the lawyers for both sides (or in some states, the judge) question all of the potential jurors to make sure that they are not biased in some way that will affect their judgement about the case. For example, they might be related to someone involved in the case, or have read newspaper articles about the crime and have already made up their minds, or they might have preconceived notions about some aspect of the case that could keep them from being open-minded. For example, a dog lover might be too biased to hear a case about a dog bite if he or she believed that a dog would never under any circumstances bite unless provoked.

Here, jurors consider the evidence in a long-running murder trial. Jurors must decide whether or not the defendant is innocent or guilty after hearing all the facts in the case. It is a responsibility that they should take very seriously.

Robert Noel and his wife Marjorie Knoller were convicted of involuntary manslaughter after their dogs attacked and killed a neighbor, Diane Whipple. Knoller, who was present at the attack, was also convicted of second-degree murder. That conviction was overturned on appeal because the appellate judge said there was no evidence to show that Knoller knew her dogs would attack and kill. Both Knoller and Noel were sentenced to four years in prison for manslaughter.

The lawyers on either side can reject a certain number of jurors without saying why: this is called a peremptory challenge. They can also reject as many other jurors as they like, but they have to explain why and the judge must agree that it is for a good reason. This is called challenge for cause. In a murder case, cause might be that a juror's close relative or friend had been murdered, with the result that the juror may believe that someone accused of murder was likely to be guilty. A juror's race or sex can never be the reason he or she is excluded.

Selecting the right jury is important to the strategy of the two legal teams. Both the prosecution and the defense want to select a jury that is likely to be more sympathetic to their side. The number of jurors selected (empanelled) varies from state to state, and sometimes according to the severity of the crime. When the jurors and alternates have been selected, the trial can begin.

COURT APPEARANCES

After someone has been arrested, he or she must be brought before a court as soon as possible to be charged. Assuming the crime is a felony, the following stages occur. At the first hearing, the judge makes sure that a crime has been committed and that the prosecution has enough evidence

THE APPELLATE PROCESS

A guilty verdict is not necessarily the end of the story. The defense lawyers will order a transcript of the trial so that they can review the judge's rulings during the case and try to find places where the judge got the law wrong. If they find that the judge did something wrong, they can appeal to a higher court to have the decision reversed, or to get a new trial. Some cases have been appealed all the way to the Supreme Court.

to show that the defendant committed it. If there is not enough evidence, the accused has to be released. However, he or she can be arrested again later if the police find more evidence. If there is enough evidence, the case is continued. "Bound over" refers to transferring the case to a higher trial court or a trial court that hears felonies. The first court a defendant goes to is usually a general **arraignment** court, which hears misdemeanors.

Bail arrangements may also be made at this time. Bail is a sum of money held by the court to make sure that the defendant appears at the trial. The judge sets the amount based on the seriousness of the crime and the likelihood that the person will try to run away. In some states, bail can be refused if the defendant is thought to be a danger to the public; in other states, bail is simply a bond to ensure the defendant's appearance at court. The defendant can also be released on his own recognizance; that is, on his word that he will appear in court. If the defendant does not appear in court when she is supposed to, she loses any money posted (the bond), a warrant is taken out for her arrest, and when she is found, she is usually taken to jail to await trial. Failure to appear is a separate crime for which she may also be charged.

The next stage is the indictment. This is the formal accusation of the defendant. In about half the states and in all federal cases, the accused is indicted by a grand jury. A grand jury is a panel of citizens who meet to decide if the accused should stand trial. If they decide to indict, they pass a verdict of "true bill." If they decide there is not enough evidence to indict, they bring in a verdict of "no bill." At a grand jury hearing, only the prosecution's case is heard. The defendant does not have a lawyer present and, due to the Fifth Amendment right not to incriminate himself, the defendant does not usually give evidence in a grand jury hearing. Since grand juries hear only the prosecution's side of the case, they usually bring in an indictment. In the words of one lawyer, a grand jury would indict a ham sandwich if the prosecutor told them to. In states that do not use grand juries, the accused is indicted by information at a preliminary

PREJUDICIAL PUBLICITY

If there has been a lot of pre-trial publicity about a case, the defense may argue that a fair trial is impossible and the judge may order the case to be moved to another town where it is less well known. In a recent California case—a woman killed by two dogs in San Francisco—the defense argued that a fair trial was impossible due to extensive coverage by newspapers and on TV. The judge agreed, and the case was moved to Los Angeles. One of the defendants was convicted of second-degree manslaughter. Here, the prosecution team arrives at the courthouse.

Judges make decisions throughout the course of a trial. Here, Judge William D. Mudd makes a ruling about what can be admitted into evidence at a murder trial.

hearing. This means that the prosecutor swears that there is enough evidence to indict.

At the arraignment, the judge notifies the accused of the charges and asks how he or she pleads. The accused might plead *nolo contendere* (Latin for "I will not contest"), also called "no contest." This is not an admission of guilt. The defendant may also plead guilty under the Alford doctrine, named for the *North Carolina v. Alford* case. In this type of plea, the defendant agrees that the state probably has enough evidence to convict, but that he still insists he is not guilty. If the accused enters an Alford plea or pleads "*nolo contendere*" or "guilty" to the charges, there is no trial. Instead, the judge moves directly to the sentencing. If the charge is a felony, the case is continued for sentencing so that a pre-sentence investigation report may be prepared for the judge. If the accused pleads not guilty, then there is a trial to find out if he or she is guilty or not.

THE PRETRIAL PERIOD

Now the two sides go away to prepare their cases. During this period, there might be a pretrial conference, so the two sides can meet to decide if there is anything they can agree on. If the plea is not guilty by reason of insanity in a murder case, for example, both sides might agree that the accused did indeed kill the victim. That saves time in the trial and lets the court focus on the real point of the case: was the defendant sane or not at the time of the murder?

Both sides also file **motions**. For example, if there has been a lot of publicity about the case on television or in the newspapers, the defense might ask for the case to be moved to a different city so that the defendant can get a fair trial.

The two sides have to tell each other which witnesses they are calling, as well as what evidence they will be presenting. Unlike on television, there are no surprise witnesses. The state must provide the defendant with all the material that it has that might be helpful to the defense's case. This material

CLARENCE DARROW

One of the most famous criminal lawyers, Clarence Darrow (below) represented Leopold and Loeb and helped them avoid the electric chair despite being convicted for killing a boy for fun.

Before witnesses are allowed to testify, they must promise to tell the truth, the whole truth, and nothing but the truth. In the early years of the United States, they swore on a Bible, but now most witnesses simply promise to tell the truth.

is called the Brady material and is named after a case heard in the U.S. Supreme Court in 1963 (*Brady v. Maryland*).

Before the trial, the two sides might discuss a plea bargain. The defendant might decide to plead guilty if the prosecution offers a lesser charge or a lighter sentence. Plea bargains make sense for the prosecution because they guarantee a conviction and save time and money. They make sense for the defendant if the prosecution's case is strong and a conviction seems likely. Pleading guilty to a lesser crime means that the punishment will be less severe. A large number of criminal cases are settled in this way.

Maps, charts, and photographs are used to help the jurors understand what happened. Here, a witness at a murder trial points to the place a key conversation occurred. The judge, jury, and other court officials are often required to absorb a huge amount of information in the course of a long or complicated trial.

PRESENTING THE EVIDENCE

At the trial, both sides present their evidence. The prosecution begins by making an opening statement, outlining the case against the defendant. The state has to prove that the accused committed the crime; the accused does not have to prove that he is innocent. Then, the defense has a chance to make their opening statement. They explain what their defense will be.

The prosecution begins by calling their witnesses and producing any

A member of a jury takes notes as a police officer gives evidence while questioned by the prosecuting lawyer in a robbery trial.

The police take photographs of evidence such as this gun. Information about the evidence makes up part of the photo, as does a ruler, so that the object's size is clear.

evidence against the accused. After the prosecution has questioned the witness, a process known as direct examination, the defense gets to ask questions. This is called cross-examination. They try to show that the witness's testimony is invalid in some way.

During direct examination, only open-ended questions can be asked, such as "What did you see after you heard the shots?" Leading questions, which are questions that suggest the answer, are not allowed. If the lawyer asks a leading question, such as "Did you see John after you heard the shots?" the other side may object. The judge will either sustain (agree with) the objection and ask for the question to be struck from the record, or overrule the objection and allow the question to be asked. If something is struck from the record, the jury is told not to pay attention to it. Sometimes lawyers say things that they know will later be struck from the record because they know that despite the judge's instructions for them to forget it and the jury's best intentions, it is hard to forget something once you have heard it. If the judge thinks that the lawyer is doing this, she will warn him to stop. Leading questions are not allowed on direct examination. They are, however, allowed during the cross-examination.

EXHIBITS

Physical evidence, known as exhibits, are usually also produced to support both the prosecution and defense cases. Evidence can be an object, like a weapon or a cast of a footprint, or identifying marks, like scars or tattoos. Or it might be scientific reports or documents, such as photographs, letters, or birth certificates. Sometimes, to better understand the case, the jury is taken to view the scene of the crime or some other relevant place.

During the course of the trial, both sides may raise relevant points of law about the admissibility of the evidence or other issues. Sometimes, the jury is sent out of the room so that the two sides can make arguments about admitting a certain piece of evidence. At other times, the judge will ask the lawyers to approach the bench and they will discuss the matter quietly. The jury is instructed to ignore anything they hear during these discussions, because it is not part of the evidence in the trial.

The defense presents its case when the prosecution rests (finishes its arguments). They might try to show that the accused could not have committed the crime for some reason, such as that he or she was somewhere else at the time the crime was committed (known as an alibi). The prosecution cross-examines each witness when the defense is finished. They try to show that what the witness said is not true or to cast doubt on what the witness said.

The defendant can appear as a witness in the trial (testify), but he does not have to. This is because the Constitution says that the accused cannot be forced to incriminate himself. If the defendant chooses to testify, he is questioned and cross-examined like any other witness, and because he is under oath, he must tell the truth, even if it might harm his case. If the defendant decides not to testify, the jury is not allowed to take this as a sign that he is guilty. Later, when the judge instructs the jury at the close of the case, she will tell the jury that the defendant does not have to testify and that they should not infer anything from a decision not to testify.

When both sides have rested their cases, they present their closing arguments. The prosecution explains to the jury how they have proved the defendant's guilt beyond a reasonable doubt. The defense speaks next. They point out any holes in the prosecution's argument, such as inconsistencies between what the witnesses said, or other explanations for the evidence. The defense attorney shows all the places in the prosecution's argument where a reasonable person could find room for doubt.

The judge then instructs the jury. The judge tells them how to apply the law to the case, but does not tell them how to decide the case. The verdict is up to the jury.

THE VERDICT

The jury leaves the courtroom to make their decision. They are taken to the jury room to consider the case, a process known as deliberating. First, they elect a foreman to lead them. He or she makes sure that all the members of the jury get a chance to speak. If the jury has any questions, they are put in writing and sent to the judge by the foreman. During the deliberations, the members of the jury are not allowed to talk to anyone about the case or to watch, read, or listen to any news reports on the case. In some highly sensitive cases, the jury is sequestered during its deliberations, which means that they are kept isolated, usually in a hotel.

The verdict must be unanimous, which means that everyone on the jury must agree on it. If they cannot agree, it is called a hung jury, and there will have to be a new trial. If the jury finds the defendant not guilty, he or she goes free and can never be tried for that crime again. This is according to the Constitution's Fifth Amendment, which prevents double jeopardy.

The witnesses in a trial are questioned by lawyers from both sides. After they give their evidence, they are cross-examined by the lawyer from the other side, who tries to pick holes in what they have previously told the court.

Jurors are not allowed to discuss the case during the trial, but after it is over, they sometimes choose to talk to the press about their decision. This jury, led by their forewoman, is speaking to the media after finding a defendant guilty of involuntary manslaughter.

(The defendant may, however, face a civil suit for having wronged the victim.) If the jury finds the defendant guilty, the judge will then decide what punishment (sentence) to give out. Sometimes, juries find the defendant guilty on a lesser charge. For example, in a murder case, the jury might conclude that the defendant is guilty of manslaughter, not murder, because although he did kill the victim, he did not intend to do so. The intention to kill is an element of the crime of murder, but not of the crime of manslaughter.

SENTENCING

If the accused is found guilty, the judge does not usually hand down the sentence right away. The sentencing hearing often takes place some time later. Different people, in some states including the victim, can tell the judge what they think the sentence should be, but the final decision is up to the judge. In some states and for some crimes, there are mandatory sentences. If that is so, these are the sentences the judge must hand out. Sometimes, there are minimum and maximum sentences, and if so, the judge uses these as guidelines.

Criminal Slang

Criminal gangs often use slang. Having a special language has two main functions: it reinforces the identity of the gang and it acts like a secret language, preventing outsiders from understanding the gang members. Some American gangs, like the Mafia, use words from another language, such as "capo," which is Italian for "head" or "boss." Other gangs—for example, the British underworld—use English, but have created secret meanings for ordinary words with their rhyming slang, such as jam jar, meaning car.

Some criminal slang enters the ordinary language, made popular by movies or TV shows. Slang then finds its way into the conversation of ordinary people, as well as gang members. Such Mafia terms as beef (complaint), whack (murder), goombah (pal), ice (murder), hitting the mattresses (going into combat with a rival), wiseguy (mob member), piece (gun), and stand-up guy (someone who is loyal to the gang, no matter what) have become part of ordinary speech. Inner-city gang slang is often used in popular music, so terms such as homey (friend), slap up (hit), dis (disrespect or insult), and drive-by (shooting from a car window) are all well known.

ORGANIZED CRIME

Interpol defines organized crime as, "Any enterprise or group of persons engaged in a continuing illegal activity which has as its primary purpose the generation of profits." These groups are well organized and often have complex rules or codes of behavior. Their membership might span the

Left: Hundreds of Hell's Angels roaring by on their motorcycles is a menacing sight. These bikers, however, are on their way to the funeral of one of their members who was killed when his bike crashed in a road accident.

globe, as is the case with the Chinese Triads, or it might have spread from city to city around the United States, as did the Los Angeles gangs the Bloods and the Crips.

Organized crime is found in countries all around the world. Italy has its Mafia or Cosa Nostra, Japan has its Yakuza, China and Hong Kong have their Triads. Jamaica has its Yardies, Russia has its gangs, and South America has its drug cartels. In the United States, homegrown gangs, including inner-city gangs like the Bloods and Crips, the Hell's Angels motorcycle gang, and white supremacist gangs, coexist with gangs that originally had their roots outside the United States, such as the Mafia, the Triads, and the Yakuza. All gangs make their money through criminal activities, such as racketeering, fraud, car theft, robbery, drug dealing,

During a police search in London's Chinatown, weapons, including guns and knives, were found. This police officer holds up two large machete-style knives.

RHYMING SLANG

British criminals, many based in the East End of London, have long used rhyming slang to talk openly about their criminal activities without being understood.

"Half inch" is rhyming slang for "pinch" ("steal"), "dog and bone" means "phone," while a "tea leaf" is a "thief." In addition, they use ordinary slang, like "Old Bill" ("police"), "nick" ("arrest"), "manor" ("neighborhood"), "governor" ("boss"), "gaff" ("home"), or "drinker" ("pub"). Two of Britain's most famous Cockney criminals were violent twins Reggie and Ronnie Kray (pictured, left and right), who terrorized the East End in the '50s and '60s before being arrested.

Among graffiti artists, crossing out another's work is a serious insult. Sometimes, they use violence to avenge the insult. When a rival sprayed over Ione Cardona's tag, Cardona stabbed him to death.

selling guns, gambling, extortion, and prostitution. Some are also involved in smuggling, whether of goods or illegal aliens. All are essentially violent and antisocial.

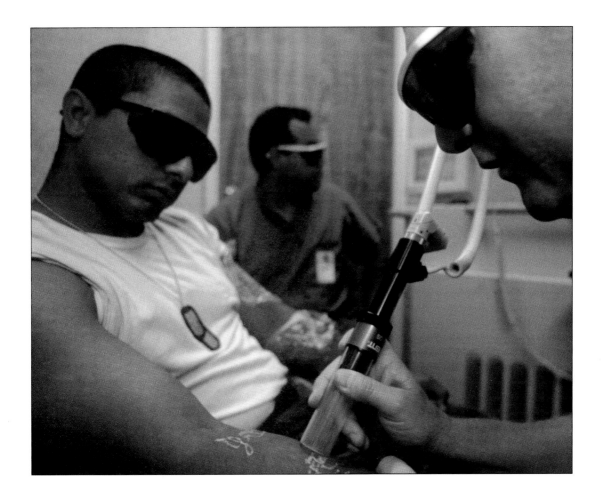

When gang members leave the gang, they sometimes have their gang tattoos burned off, as here. Prisons offer this treatment as part of their efforts to rehabilitate gang members.

INNER-CITY GANGS

Although some gangs, like the Mafia and the Yakuza, have been around for hundreds of years, other gangs have established themselves in only a few decades. U.S. gangs started with the Bloods and the Crips, two groups from rival high schools in Compton, California. Red was the school color for the Bloods, while the Crips' school color was blue.

Since the late '60s, these gangs have spread from Los Angeles to around the country and now have branches in many U.S. cities. Dozens of gangs run along similar lines also exist. Gangs are often made up of people of the same race or ethnic group, so there are black gangs, Hispanic gangs, white gangs, and Asian gangs. Although sometimes run by adults, the gangs

This police officer in Illinois examines bullets from a .22-caliber revolver that a 12-year-old boy took to school. The police were called after the boy was found showing the gun to friends. The boy was subsequently arrested.

usually recruit teenagers, particularly those who feel that they have no stake in society or even in their own families. The gang offers a sense of security, belonging, and family, but at a high price. Gang members must accept a life of crime and violence. Many are hurt or killed in gang warfare. And once a person has joined a gang, he cannot just quit, but must remain a member for life.

When someone joins a gang, he is initiated by being beaten, called being "jumped in." He then chooses a gang name and becomes part of the gang, what is known as a gang-banger. Gang names often describe appearance, habits, or personality. Gang members belong to a crew, or set (neighborhood gang). Gang members are expected to be "down for," or 100 percent behind, each other and the gang. The punishment for "ratting," or telling on others, is severe.

Gangs create a strong sense of group identity through what they wear and how they communicate. They usually wear the same clothes, such as particular brands of shoes or particular styles of clothing. The gang color may form part of the outfit. They might also use signs, such as rolling up the right pants leg, or hand signs to signal their identity. Some gang members also wear jackets or sweatshirts with the gang sign, or have gang tattoos.

David Lewis, who was involved in a battle between two rival Yardie gangs, was acquitted of killing a member of a Yardie gang in February 2002. Warfare between Yardie gangs is a very common occurrence.

Turf, or territory, is highly important to gangs. To show that a part of town belongs to them, they "tag" buildings, writing their gang name or sign on them. In disputed areas, other gangs deface the tags, crossing them out and writing their own gang name. This is often called a cross-out or "puto mark." Graffiti can also be used as a threat. For example, "187 Lil' Moe," is a death threat against someone named Lil' Moe. The police code for murder is 187.

Guns, called "pieces," including "9 Mikes" (9-mm handgun), "deuce and a half" (.25-caliber automatic), "double deuces" (.22-caliber), and "tray eights" (.38-caliber) are bought with the proceeds of drug deals. Gangs have wreaked mayhem in many neighborhoods, killing hundreds of people, many of them innocent bystanders to drive-by shootings.

BIKER GANGS

Motorcycle gangs are another **indigenous** American gang movement. The Hell's Angels are the best known. They originally started in Fontana, California, but now have branches across the United States, Canada, and in 22 countries around the world. Other large biker gangs, all of which are "at war" with the Hell's Angels, are the Outlaws, based in Chicago; the Pagans, from the East Coast; and the Bandidos, originally from Houston, Texas, but now widespread across the South and the Northwest.

Biker gangs make money from drug dealing and smuggling, estimated by the FBI as about $1 billion per year worldwide for the Hell's Angels. Violence flares up regularly in inter-gang rivalries. They use guns and explosives to settle scores.

THE MAFIA

In Italy, the Mafia is made up of three different regional organized-crime groups based in the south of Italy: the Camorra in Naples, the 'Ndrangheta in Calabria, and the Mafia in Sicily. All three have strong clan-based structures, traditions of secrecy, and codes of honor. Italian immigrants

Elaborate tattoos and gang-related clothing show that this man is a member of a biker gang.

These symbols reinforce a member's identity as part of the gang.

brought this crime structure to the United States, where, despite the efforts of the police and the FBI, it continues to flourish. It is usually called the Mafia, the Mob, or the *Cosa Nostra* (meaning "Our Thing" in Italian).

The Mafia code of silence ("omerta") makes it difficult for law enforcement authorities to convict mobsters of their crimes. Mob members

(called "wise guys" or "made men") will not testify against each other because they know the punishment is death (being "iced" or "whacked"), while members of the public are often intimidated into silence. Many mobsters have been sent to prison, not for crimes of violence, but for breaking the tax laws.

Mario Puzo's book, *The Godfather*, was made into a series of movies about the activities and lives of an Italian-American crime family headed by Don Vito Corleone, here played by Marlon Brando (second from left), and his sons.

Mafia chief John Gotti (1940–2002) was acquitted many times (including at this trial in 1990). This earned him the nickname "The Teflon Don," but he was finally convicted of murdering and racketeering and he ended his days in a federal prison.

The Mafia is organized into families (borgatas or brugads), with a leader, the don or capo. He has an advisor, the consigliere. The mobsters reporting to the capo are called soldiers, and make up a crew. Mobsters are involved in gambling, prostitution, drug dealing, and fraud. Mario Puzo's book *The Godfather* and the series of movies of the same name, as well as the television show *The Sopranos,* have made the activities and language of the Mafia well known.

RUSSIAN CRIME GANGS

The former Soviet Union is a hotbed of gang activity. Under Communism, gangs controlled the black market. With the fall of the Communist system, gangs have become widespread. They extort money from businesses and control drug sales, prostitution, and the black market. Some gang members have immigrated to the United States, where they prey on Russian immigrant communities. Some of these gangs live by a set of rules, the *Vorov v Zakone,* or thieves' code. They are organized into small groups of four cells led by a boss, or "pakhan." Each cell is run by a bridgadier. Other Russian gangs have a less rigid structure.

THE TRIADS

From their beginnings as secret societies or brotherhoods in China, the Triads have spread into Hong Kong and around the world from Chinatown to Chinatown. The Triads control much of the heroin produced in Southeast Asia and are, therefore, both wealthy and powerful. In many cities, they operate by extorting money from businesses. They are also involved in traditional gang activities, such as gambling and prostitution.

THE YAKUZA

Japan's criminal gangs have a history going back centuries to three groups of criminals: the *Bakuto,* or gamblers from feudal Japan; the *Gurentai,* or hoodlums who controlled the black market in postwar Japan; and the

This man was jailed as a member of a Triad "Snakehead" organization for being involved in extorting money and smuggling drugs into Britain.

This ammunition magazine was seized in a raid on London's Chinatown. Triad members prey upon the Chinese community, often extorting money from them in exchange for so-called "protection."

Tekiya, or street pedlars. Yakuza is a catchall term for these gangsters, although the police often call them *Boroyokudan*, which literally means "violence groups."

Like many gangs, the Yakuza are organized into families, with more experienced members (*oyabun*, or parent) training younger members (*kobun*, or child). Strict discipline is maintained, and if a member is disobedient, he can be ordered to slice off the first joint of his little finger, a ritual called *yubitsume*. The two largest crime syndicates in Japan are the *Yamaguchi-gumi* and the *Sumiyoshi-rengo*. They are also active outside Japan.

GLOSSARY

Appeal: the referral of a case to a higher court for review

Arraignment: the hearing at which the accused is notified of the charges and asked how he pleads

Arson: the deliberate burning (or attempted burning) of a building

Book (v.): to enter charges against a person in a police register

Circumstantial evidence: evidence that tends to prove a fact by proving other events or circumstances which afford a basis for a reasonable inference of the occurrence of the fact at issue

Electron microscope: an instrument that focuses a beam of electrons—particles of an atom—to enlarge a minute object

Embezzlement: stealing of any form of property (including money) by a person to whom it has been entrusted—a bank clerk, for example

Felony: the most serious category of crime, carrying a penalty of more than one year in jail

Fine (v.): to punish someone by making him pay a sum for an offense

Forensics: the scientific analysis and review of the physical and medical evidence of a crime

Frisk: to search an individual (usually by the police)

Indigenous: growing, living, or occurring naturally in a particular region or environment

Interpol: an association of national police forces that promotes cooperation and mutual assistance in apprehending international criminals and criminals who flee abroad to avoid justice

Jurisdiction: the power or right to exercise authority

Legislature: an organized body that has the authority to make laws.

Misdemeanor: a lesser crime, punishable by under one year in jail

Motion: an application for a court order, made while the case is in progress

Reasonable doubt: standard of proof used in a criminal case—not absolute certainty, but a proof that stands up to common-sense objections

Vice: moral depravity or corruption

CHRONOLOGY

1775–1783:   Revolutionary War.

1776:   Declaration of Independence is signed.

1787:   Constitutional Convention meets in Philadelphia, Pennsylvania; December 7, Delaware becomes the first state to ratify the Constitution.

1790:   May 29, Rhode Island becomes the last state to ratify the Constitution.

1791:   December 15, Bill of Rights is ratified.

1803:   February 24, Supreme Court decision in *Marbury v. Madison* creates principle of judicial review.

1870:   Department of Justice is created.

1908:   Federal Bureau of Investigation (FBI) is established.

1914:   In *Weeks v. United States*, the Supreme Court rules that without a warrant, evidence found during a search cannot be used in court.

1919:   January 16, 18th Amendment is ratified, establishing Prohibition by forbidding the sale of intoxicating liquors.

1920:   August 18, 19th Amendment is ratified, giving women the right to vote.

1932:   FBI Crime Lab opens.

1933:   December 5, 21st Amendment is ratified, repealing Prohibition (18th Amendment).

1939:   *Nardone v. United States* establishes the "Fruit of the Poisonous Tree" doctrine, which excludes evidence derived from the results of an illegal search.

1961:   Supreme Court decision of *Mapp v. Ohio* rules that evidence seized in violation of Fourth Amendment rights is inadmissible.

1966:   Supreme Court decision of *Miranda v. Arizona* states that if police do not inform suspects of their rights before they arrest them, they cannot use what they say as evidence in court.

1972:   Supreme Court decision of *Furman v. Georgia* bans the death penalty because of violations of due-process procedures.

1974:   Supreme Court decision of *Gregg v. Georgia* reinstitutes the death penalty with new procedures.

1987:   Federal government passes Victims of Crimes Act.

1995:   O.J. Simpson is acquitted of the murders of Nicole Brown Simpson and Ronald Goldman after spending $6 million on his defense.

FURTHER INFORMATION

Useful Web Sites

www.abanet.org: American Bar Association

www.cjcj.org: Center on Juvenile and Criminal Justice

www.courttv.com: Court TV Web site

www.fbi.gov: FBI's Web site

www.findlaw.com: Opinions and resources on the Supreme Court

www.inter-law.com: Legal encyclopedia and dictionary

www.law.indiana.edu: A virtual legal library

www.lectlaw.com: An online law library

www.uscourts.gov: Federal judiciary Web site

www.ycwa.org: Youth Crime Watch

Further Reading

Atkin, Beth. *Voices from the Streets: Young Former Gang Members Tell Their Stories.* Boston: Little Brown and Company, 1996.

Bintliff, Russell. *Police Procedural: A Writer's Guide to the Police and How They Work.* Cincinnati, Ohio: Writer's Digest Books, 1993.

Boland, Mary L. *Crime Victim's Guide to Justice.* Naperville, IL: Sourcebooks, 1997.

Calvi, James V. and Susan Coleman. *American Law and Legal Systems.* Englewood Cliff, N.J.: Prentice Hall, 1989.

Gardner, Robert. *Crime Lab 101: Experimenting with Crime and Detection.* New York: Walker, 1992.

Irving, Shae and Kathleen Michon (Eds.). *Nolo's Encyclopedia of Everyday Law: Answers to Your Most Frequently Asked Legal Questions.* Berkeley, CA: Nolo Press, 1996.

Jeffreys, Diarmiud. *The Bureau: Inside the Modern FBI.* Boston: Houghton Mifflin, 1995.

Kaplan, David E. and Alec Dubro. *Yakuza: The Explosive Account of Japan's Criminal Underworld.* New York: Collier Books, 1987.

Mauro, Tony. *Illustrated Great Decisions of the Supreme Court.* Washington, D.C.: CQ Press, 2000.

Newman, Roger K., Editor-in-Chief. *The Constitution and Its Amendments.* New York: Macmillan Reference, 1999.

Silverstein, Herma. *Threads of Evidence: Using Forensic Science to Solve Crimes.* New York: 21st Century Books, a division of Henry Holt & Co., 1996.

Ventura, John. *Law For Dummies.* Foster City, CA: IDG Books Worldwide, 1996.

About the Author

Ellen Dupont has written on a wide variety of subjects, mostly for publishers of illustrated books, such as Reader's Digest, Time Life Books, Dorling Kindersley Books, and Grolier. Having edited several health books, Ellen began writing on health and has either contributed to or ghostwritten a number of health titles. In addition to general consumer health subjects, Ellen specializes in food and nutrition. She has run children's cookery classes and adapted recipes from around the world for children.

Ellen has written three books on consumer rights and the law: *The U.S. Judicial System, Criminal Terminology,* and *Fair Recruitment and Selection.* The first two were written for young adults and explain the principles and practices of the American legal system to high school students. *Fair Recruitment and Selection* is a guide for managers, covering equal opportunities policies, creating a job specification, interviewing and assessment, and candidate selection. Other topics that Ellen has written on are the paranormal, mythology, movie stars, and pets.

A native of Connecticut and a graduate of Brown University, Ellen lives in London, England, with her husband and son.

INDEX